PREPARATION:
a spiritual journey

*For, verily, in the remembrance of God
do hearts find their rest*
(Quran 13:28)

PREPARATION:
a spiritual journey

Sakina A.

First published in the UK by Beacon Books and Media Ltd
Earl Business Centre, Dowry Street, Oldham OL8 2PF, UK.

Copyright © Sakina A. 2025

The right of Sakina A. to be identified as the author of this work has been asserted in accordance with the Copyright, Designs and Patents Act 1988. All rights reserved. This book may not be reproduced, scanned, transmitted or distributed in any printed or electronic form or by any means without the prior written permission from the copyright owners, except in the case of brief quotations embedded in critical reviews and other non-commercial uses permitted by copyright law.

First edition published in 2025

www.beaconbooks.net

ISBN 978-1-916955-69-1 Paperback
ISBN 978-1-916955-70-7 Ebook

Cataloging-in-Publication record for this book is available from the British Library

Cover design by Raees Mahmood Khan

Contents

Prologue vii

Blessings 2
A Tree Called *Deen* 3
Faith 4
Awakening 5
Sign 6
The Pain of Separation 8
Connections 9
Rahma 10
Love 11
Thank You 12
Prayer Beads 14
There He Was 15
Tawheed 16
Fruit 17
Tahajjud 18
Kindling a Fire 19
Longing 22
This One Man 23
To Muhammad ﷺ 24
Muhammad ﷺ 25
Yearning 26
My Ego and Relationships 28
Ascension 29
Anxiety 31
Ramadan 34
Holiday 36
Cleaning 37
Mama 38
I'm Sorry 40
Summer 41

Power 42
Time 43
Diamond 44
Development 45
Friendship 48
Rainclouds 50
Broken 51
Friday 52
He Lost 53
Tawbah 56
My Son 57

Glossary 60

Prologue

These poems reflect the spiritual journey I have taken over the past 20 years since becoming Muslim. I feel the path I must travel is only now becoming clear. So far, I have packed my bag in preparation, readying myself for the quest of self-improvement and seeking closeness to God.

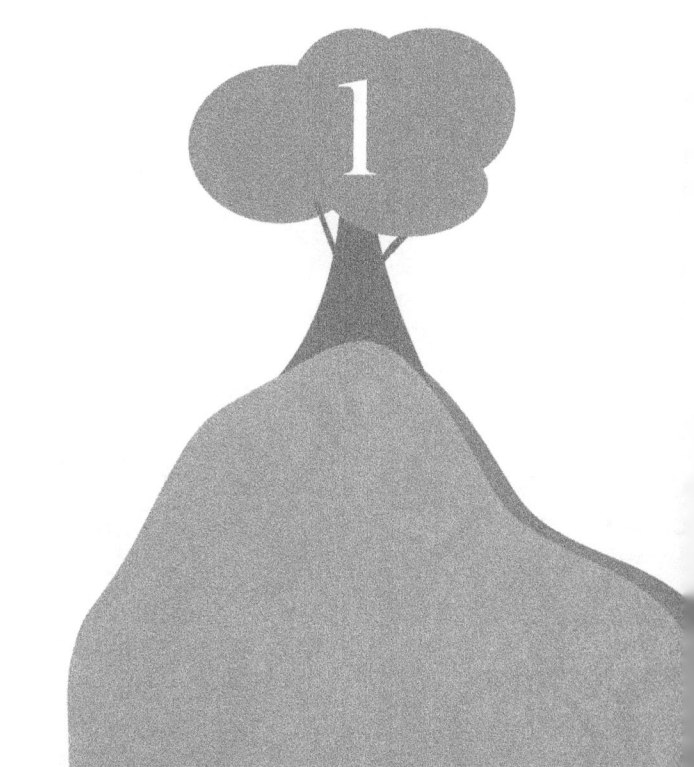

1
The Beginning of the Journey

Blessings

Mother
Father
Stepmother
Stepfather
Brother
Half-brother
Grandmother
Childhood
Night
Moon
Stars
Hands
Eyes
Ears
Smell
Farm
Cat
Horse
Walking
Rolling hills
Blue sky
Clouds
Nor'wester
Finding God

A Tree Called *Deen*

I was gifted a seed
to the most beautiful tree,
so I planted it deep within.

I watered it
and gave it light
until a seedling sprung.

The seedling was rejected
by those nearest,
afraid of the unknown.

I sheltered and protected it
against the words of the storm
that lashed outside.

Its roots held firm
and allowed the sapling
to sway and find its path.

The tree, too strong
for the axe of words
which tired with each swing.

The mature tree,
with its sheltering leaves,
softened the hearts of those nearby.

This beautiful tree,
rooted deep within,
is the tree called *Deen*.

Faith

How do I describe
what now lies inside,
replacing the emptiness,
filling my chest with bliss:
contentment,
satisfaction,
warmth,
love.

Faith

Awakening

I tasted the sweetest honey,
it awoke me from a dream.
I looked around and saw
others still sound asleep.

I wanted to drag
the slumbering from their daze,
so they could experience
true rest in the arms of God.

Each soul is suffering
in its distance from God.
Don't they know they have a Lord who loves them—
unconditionally, just as they are?

Ask forgiveness from your Lord and repent to Him.
Verily, my Lord is Merciful and Loving.
(Quran 11:90)

Sign

'My Lord,' I cry, 'Show me a sign.
Let me see an angel. Help calm my mind.'
How foolish was I?
This sinful soul
with a head so full—
arrogant.
Who am I?
To think myself high?
When in reality,
my questioning
was in keeping
with the *kufar*.

If I opened my eyes, I would see,
and that, in itself, a mercy,
a gift,
a sign.
Miracles everywhere I look
yet I mistook
an angel in the sky
as a way to certify
Your love
and existence.
Oh, how very wrong
was I.

My Lord, forgive me.

2

Seeking Allah's Nearness

The Pain of Separation

There's an ache,
a void,
an emptiness.

A sense
of something missing,
of loneliness.

Unable to be filled
by adrenaline, consumption,
or anything

other
than
God.

He created the pain
of separation,
so we search

and
return
to God.

Connections

Connecting
to the One
in the heavens above
is an experience
greater than love.

Yet,
how many lovers
remain with arms wide open
when forgotten
and ignored?

How can I
continue to ignore
My Lord, *Al Wadud*,
when He allowed me
to experience
a moment of His love?

The One
who is waiting
for me
to reach out,
call on Him
and be grateful.

The One
who will rush towards me
if I just take a few steps to Him.
O Most Merciful, forgive me,
and bring me back
to You.

Rahma

Your mercy,
Rahma,
an unconditional love,
flows from a limitless source.

I dance
with joy
in the discovery of
a run-off stream.

A sip from this stream
overwhelms my heart
clears its vessels
making it beat strong once again.

Yet,
I crave more.
I want to follow the stream
to its source.

I want to indulge
in the water
as I journey
back to God.

O Allah,
make me love You,
experience Your love,
as much as You love me.

Love

My loving, caring Lord,
I can't believe how much
you love me.

Waiting for me to think of You,
and remembering me if I do.
You are closer than my own self,
and if I come to you, You come to me,
Yourself—
but in a much more beautiful, elevated way.
O my Lord I yearn for the day
that I finally get to see You,
although I will be seen through
my soul laid bare,
my deeds I fear,
inadequate.

I know with certainty You won't forsake me,
for You are *Ar-Rahman*
and Your mercy
overcomes
Your anger.

Allow me to dwell
in Your presence
forever.

Thank You

How can I show
appreciation to
the One who
creates,
sustains,
and nourishes
every organism?

How can I show
gratitude to
the Lord above, who
created my mind
and taught me
how to use it?

How can I
begin to understand
the subtle ways
my Lord's hand
guides, teaches
and blesses me?

How can I thank
the Lord
who created all,
upon whom everything depends—
yet He depends
on nothing.

How can I—
this one of many,
but special to You—

really
truly
say: 'thank you'?

My words fall short.

My Lord,

Thank You.

Prayer Beads

Dark brown,
scented with sandalwood,
one hundred long,
run between
my fingers and thumb.

Words of praise
follow suit.
Mind, lips, heart and hand
collectively
remember.

They lift the bedsheets
off my sleeping heart.
They pull the blinds;
rays of light stream in,
awakening.

My soul, content,
now that those blackout blinds
have been removed.
The light, a reminder
of my true purpose.

There He Was

I faltered,
and there He was—
Carrying me
until I regained
my footing

How could I falter,
when there He was
all along,
closer to me
than my jugular vein.

Tawheed

Except for Him, there is naught.
No other god or concept,
no ego or possession
that has the right
to be worshipped
except Him.

He made all.
He is the cause of creation.
His act of fashioning and formation
is not by anything or anyone
except by Him.

Every interaction with His creation
is an interaction with Him.
He has complete control,
and nothing occurs
except with His permission

Fruit

I once ate
this rare, sweet fruit
so beautiful
in taste and texture.

It can only be picked
just before dawn,
in a state of
ritual ablution.

One must get down
on her hands and knees
and open her heart
to God.

This fruit will then
appear in her chest
with its flavour lingering
on her lips.

Once savoured,
worldly fruits
are completely
out of the question.

Though rare,
if she wants more,
she just needs to get up
and answer the call.

Tahajjud

Every night there is an open invitation,
to have a conversation,
with the Lord Most High.
While others lie,
asleep in their bed,
on my knees I beg—
pleading for Your Mercy.
O, my Lord, forgive
this sinner's soul.

Thank you, my Lord,
for allowing me
to experience Thee.
Now please extend
Your inviting hand
and bring me back
for I became slack.
Laziness has hit
and I have slipped.
Please open the door,
of *tahajjud*.

The last third of the night
my Lord descends,
and is willing to spend
time with me.
Oh, I ask Thee
to allow me to wake
and from those chains, shake.
Entrain my soul
to focus its goal
on the reality
of You, My Lord.

Kindling a Fire

A light within was lit,
glowing dimly but firmly there.
I tried and tried to brighten it,
keeping it close within my care.

It stubbornly refused to enliven,
no matter how much fuel I gave.
It stayed as a little light within,
just enough to show the pave.

As I stumbled along in the shadows,
trying to stay upon the path.
I tripped and fell upon my nose,
and let out an enormous gasp.

The oxygen within my breath
allowed the flame to roar.
It scared away my soul's near death,
which was waiting at my door.

Salawat is the oxygen
that has sparked my fire to life.
It has made the *siratul mustaqeem*
clearly visible, just like broad daylight.

3

The Love of the Prophet

Longing

Rasulullah ﷺ
wished he could meet
those who believed,
those who had faith,
whose eyes had not been blessed
to rest their gaze
on *Muhammad* ﷺ.

Ya *Rasulullah* ﷺ,
your message has reached,
transformed my life,
and filled it with light.
Now count me among
those you longed to meet,
O, *Muhammad* ﷺ.

This One Man

This one man,
my Lord's beloved,
was sent with a message
for me.

This one man
suffered humiliation
and endured tribulations
for me.

This one man
taught kindness
and patience
to me.

This one man
came with a gift,
God's revelation,
for me

This one man,
more beautiful than the moon
and brighter than the sun,
has been sent
from my Lord
to me.

Ya Allah, allow me to know
Your beloved in this life
and drink from his hand
in the next.

To Muhammad ﷺ

Writing to you solidifies your reality,
a reality I acknowledged
but had not embodied.

'My dear' is how I address my loved ones,
yet you should be my loved one.
Why have I not yet addressed you as my dear?

Your presence in my life has transformed me,
your teachings were directed to me.
Why have I not yet addressed you as my dear?

You explained that *rahma* was God's unconditional love,
by showing me a mother reuniting with her child.
Why have I not addressed you as my dear?

Every week you see my deeds and ask for my forgiveness,
and I know you will do the same on the Day of Judgement.
Why have I not addressed you as my dear?

You sacrificed everything to convey God's truth,
so I could receive this message.
Why have I not addressed you as my dear?

You are God's beloved,
a manifestation of His love to humanity,
O Muhammad ﷺ, my dear.

Muhammad ﷺ

My Prophet
unparalleled in character.
He was the Beloved of God,
Al-Amin, the Trustworthy.
May God send His peace and blessings upon him.
May God allow me to meet him in this life,
and let me be his neighbour in Paradise. Amin.
Dear to us all, Muhammad ﷺ.

Yearning

A man once asked
how to see *Rasulullah* ﷺ?
His teacher showed him thirst—
he needed desire
he needed to yearn for his loved one.

Ya Rabbi
I have read his *seerah*,
listened to the *shama'il*
sent *salawat*,
but I seem to be falling short.

Ya Rabbi,
let me see his face.
One smile.
Let me meet this man
who changed history.

Ya Rabbi,
I'm thirsty,
I'm yearning.
Remove the barrier
and send him to me.

4

The Inner Struggle

My Ego and Relationships

My relationships keep breaking,
the same mistakes I keep making.
Yet, I continue to blame
and shift fault
onto the other.
When in fact,
it's me.

My *nafs*—ego,
is keeping me low.
Seeking praise
and finding ways
to place myself at the forefront.
When, in fact, others should be well in front
of this greedy soul.

The faults of my children—a reflection
of my many imperfections.
My bitterness
destroying their joyfulness.
I'm quick to lay blame,
but never take the shame
or responsibility
of my actions

Now I know
of this ego.
The fight is on,
I will be strong,
with God's help.
I can try to mend
and prevent further bends
in my relationships.

Ascension

I've been told
the *salah* is an ascension
through the seven heavens
for the believer.

Our prophet found comfort,
sacrificing his restful sleep
to be in the presence
of his Lord.

How can I beautify
this masjid that's inside,
and make it a place
I yearn to go?

I am stuck way down here
and cannot see the stairs
to find the way
up to my Lord.

It may be my full mind
and heavy heart.
Or view of the *salah*
as a burdensome task.

No, those are just excuses
to satisfy my *nafs*,
avoiding the discomfort
of making lasting change.

I just need to stop,
reflect on God's Glory

ask for His help
and He will raise me up.

—

O Allah, make my prayer an ascension,
a source of comfort and peace.
Make it a deep connection,
to You, my Lord.
Amin.

Anxiety

Something was out of place.
Each step difficult,
a tightness of breath,
heaviness filled the air.

Internal tremors,
butterflies,
clenched jaw—
my control was gone.

This anxiety,
this loss of control,
is unignorable,
and overwhelming.

Allah, Allah, Allah.
His Promise is true.
In His remembrance,
my heart calmed.

The butterflies landed.
My eyebrows softened.
The tension lifted.
The control was never mine.

5

Sacred Time and Family

Ramadan

Long awaited,
our predecessors
spent months in preparation.

Rajab planting seeds,
sown only into one
absorbed in *istaghfir*.

Sha'ban watering those seeds,
with *sawm* those plants grow,
and with *salawat* upon Muhammad ﷺ they flower.

Harvesting
the blessing of *Ramadan*
is open to those who planted.

As well as those who witness,
Ramadan—the month of mercy
from our Merciful Lord.

The absence of the whisperer,
palpable,
from the first crescent moon.

The constriction
removed from our chest.
Al Qaabid, Al Baasit expands our being

Our Lord,
in His Loving Kindness
allowed us to reach this month.

He allowed us
to be revived by the *Quran*.
Our *nafs* deprived for a few short hours.

Holiday

My holiday, a sigh of relief,
a break from the usual obligations.
No prayer or fasting can be done
during menstruation.

As time went by, I began to feel
distant from my Lord.
That week of separation
struck a delicate chord.

Surely the One Above,
who is Infinitely Loving,
wouldn't want me to forget Him—
it's not just all or nothing.

I slowly began to realise
the blessing of this time,
using remembrance and reflection
to connect to my Lord Sublime.

Cleaning

I used to hate cleaning,
all the effort and no fun.
Within an hour of completion
the work would be undone.

I used to despise cleaning,
a mindless task that never ends.
A wasteful use of time—
I had other ways to spend.

I used to dislike cleaning,
but now I've changed my way,
A clean house removes the *jinn*
and lets the angels stay.

Now I clean my house with love
knowing that I am blessing
every room and every corner.
And *Allah* knows my intention.

Mama

Kindness
carves its mark
around her eyes.

Her lips busy
whispering words
of praise.

Her hands
preparing love
to satiate others.

She cares
for her children
with *dua* and *Quran*

Her heart pure,
filled with light,
which
    overflows
and shines forth
from her face.

6

Tests, Trials and Reflections on Creation

I'm Sorry

I'm so sorry, I wish I could take away your pain,
no matter which analgesic—it will be the same.
These pills cannot heal the wound
that has come from the loss
of what was in your womb.
That life is gone. Hopes, vanished.
Your heart, shattered.

Only you can collect
those thousand tiny shards
of what was once your heart
and start the healing process.
You can glue them with gold
and etch your child's soul
into yours.

I'm so sorry, there is nothing we can do,
now please just turn to
The One, The True,
who is always there for you.
He can allow you to vanquish
and heal your anguish.
He will reunite you both
in Paradise.

Summer

Temperatures soar.
The last drop
of precious water evaporates.
Fires burn.
Forests, destroyed.

Yet among the devastation,
we hold firm to promise
that summer will end.
Rain will eventually come,
and life will rejuvenate.

We know the truth of temporality—
nothing remains the same.
God has shown us this time again.
He gives life to barren earth.
Who are we to ignore His signs?

This world has a beginning and an end.
But not *Allah*.
He is the only One who never perishes.
The fire overpowers us,
yet nothing overpowers Him.

Power

They tried
with all their might—
sent in men,
trucks,
helicopters,
ships,
for months on end.
But they could not overcome her:

Nature.

Her full fury—
burning,
engulfing,
destroying.

They forgot:
she is a creation of *Allah*.
He is in total control.

In one swift move
He sent down rain,
hail,
extinguished the fires.
He brought relief,
Renewed life.

Yet
they continued
to deny

Time

Sometimes it slips like sand though fingers.
Sometimes it pauses.
Sometimes it flows, with blossoms blooming in its wake.
Regardless, each day passed is lost, never to be regained.

Three days' work can be achieved in one,
when blessing is found in time.
An hour's work can take an entire day,
when time is devoid of blessing.

With time there are many firsts,
many lasts,
many brokens and forgottens.
Time continues to move, not waiting on anyone.

With time our problems will resolve,
and we will find new ones.
With time we forget our new problem
was born from prayers of desperation.

Time chisels its mark on faces,
dips hair in buckets of silver,
and mellows out one's rages.
Time reveals itself
through life's many stages.

Dependent infant,
lively child,
strong adult.
frail,
dependent elderly.

Ending in the beginning.

Diamond

Deep within the ground,
hidden inside the kimberlite,
I discovered a beautiful diamond,
a reflection of God's light.

The brightness of this diamond
lit up my entire being,
and allowed me to continue,
despite what I was seeing.

The ignorance of men
who thought themselves superior—
that thought, in and of itself,
made them somewhat inferior.

Their focus on the external
and that which was apparent,
with complete denial of the internal,
turned religion abhorrent.

They loved to dig within the ground,
but never reached the kimberlite.
Their focus was upon the dirt,
instead of diamonds—God's true light.

Development

One
    by
    one
    her
    petals
    fell
    to
    the
    ground.
She let them go,
released her grasp.
Their benefit now gone,
pollinators flew on by.

It seemed her beauty had disappeared,

but inside she was growing something new.

7

Community and Mercy

Friendship

With a smile,
she greeted me,
hugged me,
and welcomed into her family—
all because I was her sister in *Islam*.

I praised her shoes.
She returned
the next day
with the same pair
in my size.

Her speech
and manner
are inspired by her love
for our Prophet ﷺ
and Merciful Lord.

When I strayed,
she gently pulled me back
and lifted me up,
reminding me
of my Loving Lord.

My son's arrival
into this world
was met by her mother,
pacing the hallway
and making *dua*.

She's a gift
from my Lord,
lifting the heaviness
I didn't even realise
existed.

*May God grant her shade on the day there is no shade but His.
Amin.*

Verily, Allah will say on the Day of Resurrection: Where are those who love each other for the sake of My glory? Today, I will shelter them in My shade on a day when there is no shade but Mine.
(Sahih Muslim)

Rainclouds

The dark rainclouds extend from one horizon to the other,
leaving no space for a single ray of light.
An acute reflection on the state of my heart:
dull,
grey,
and dead without my children.

As she releases her rain,
my eyes release their tears.
Vision obscured by the thick veil
of heartache,
of longing,
from our physical separation.

My Lord's love is like that of a mother—
forever present,
always concerned,
always longing,
and waiting
for her children to return.

The rain pours down, soaking my heart and soul,
as a mercy from my Lord,
reminding me of Him,
of His loving care for me,
how He nourishes me,
and strengthens me.

I will get through this.

Broken

Those shots,
that stole away life,
also pierced holes
in the walls of hate.

The tap of mercy
turned on.
Compassion
flowing freely.

Community,
now brothers
and sisters
in humanity.

A reflection on the unintended effects of the terrorist attack in Christchurch

Friday

Darkness
Hatred
Rage
Bloodshed
Hope in humanity lost

Compassion
Flowers
Headscarves
Haka
Hope in humanity found.

He Lost

From a blackened heart,
filled with hate and rage,
a planned attack
against Muslims was made.

As the devout gathered
to remember and pray,
that dark heart recorded
his deeds that day.

He spread his darkness.
He tore families apart.
His arrogance and pride
destroyed his own heart.

Darkness exists
in the absence of light.
But those he killed
now have true clarity of sight.

New Zealand stood firm—
full of love and kindness—
a light brightly shining
into the deepest crevasse.

He didn't realise;
those martyrs died
in the best month,
on the best day,
in the best place,
remembering God—
the best end to this life.

8

Closing Reflections

Tawbah

Regret begets remorse.
Sorrow-filled tears flow.
Broken promises,
unfulfilled obligations.
Palms upturned,
begging for forgiveness.
I turn to You,
O Acceptor of Repentance,
and pray that You turn to me
with mercy.

And, O my people! Ask forgiveness of your Lord, then turn unto Him repentant; He will cause the sky to rain abundance on you and will add strength to your strength. Turn not away, guilty! (Quran 11:52)

My Son

My son, come.
Let us talk.
Let me pass on some advice,
given to me,
which I will now hand over to thee.

Your God—
He is One.
Worship Him alone.
Put nil else on a throne.
Each time you are in difficulty,
open your heart to God and you will see
that your situation is actually a blessing.
And although you were left guessing
as to the wisdom of God,
just stop,
and put your trust in God.

My son,
more important
than your appearance,
is your adherence
to good manners.
It is better than any manor
that you could buy.
Kindness and generosity,
as well as honesty are qualities
that will take you far in this life.
But you will see their true result in Paradise.
Don't let this life delude you—
it is here to seduce you.
Don't let it drag you down,

for many men have drowned,
consumed by this world.
If you find yourself being pulled down that path,
just stop and ask.
Your Lord will not forsake you.

My son,
you have a God
who is infinitely loving.
His mercy to you is greater
than that of a mother.
And as your mother I can tell you,
that His love for you transcends,
as my love for you has no end.
No matter what you do,
or where you find yourself,
remember that He loves you.
And I love you.
The door to God is always open—
the easiest to enter is that of repentance.
Just lift your hands and ask for forgiveness.
And there, you will find
your Lord,
waiting for you.

May my Lord accept this small act of devotion.
Amin

Glossary

Allah: The name of God, the One who we worship, who has no partners, and whose names and attributes are the most beautiful.

Al-Amin: *The Trustworthy*, a title given to the Prophet Muhammad ﷺ prior to prophethood.

Al-Baqii: One of the beautiful names/attributes of God meaning *The Everlasting*.

Al-Baqara: *The cow*, the second chapter of the *Quran*.

Al-Baasit: One of the beautiful names/attributes of God meaning *He who expands*.

Al-Fatiha: Translated as *The Opening*, the first chapter of the Quran.

Al-Qaabid: One of the beautiful names/attributes of God meaning *He who contracts*.

Al-Wadud: One of the beautiful names/attributes of God meaning *The Most Loving*.

Ar-Rahman: One of the beautiful names/attributes of God meaning *The Most Merciful, the unconditionally loving*.

Deen: Religion or way of life.

Dhikr: Remembrance of God.

Dua: Supplication or personal prayer to God (outside of the five formal daily prayers).

Ka'aba: The house of God, the holiest Muslim site, located in Mecca, Saudi Arabia, and the direction Muslims face in formal prayer.

Nafs: The lower soul/self that responds to desires.

Rahma: Mercy; the Prophet Muhammad ﷺ explained *Rahma* to his companions as a mother's unconditional love.

Rajab: The 7th month of the Islamic calendar; one of the four sacred months. A month Muslims often seek forgiveness.

Ramadan: The 9th month of the Islamic calendar, during which all able-bodied adult Muslims fast for the entire month.

Rasulullah: A title given to the Prophet Muhammad ﷺ, meaning *Messenger of God*.

Salah: The five formal daily prayers, both physical and spiritual, performed by Muslims.

Salawat: Sending peace and blessings upon the Prophet Muhammad ﷺ; a form of prayer where God sends multiple blessings on the person sending *salawat*.

Sawm: Fasting from food and drink from dawn until sunset.

Seerah: The events during the life of the Prophet Muhammad ﷺ.

Sha'ban: The 8th month of the Islamic calendar, often spent with extra fasting and sending salawat upon the Prophet.

Shama'il: The description of the appearance, characteristics, and manners of the Prophet Muhammad ﷺ.

Siratul Mustaqeem: *The Straight Path*, a reference to Islam.

Surah: A chapter of the *Quran*.

Tahajjud: The additional prayer offered in the early hours before dawn.

Tawbah: Repentance.

Tawheed: The concept of God's oneness, that He has no partners or children.

Ya Rabbi: *O my Lord*, a call upon God using His loving names and attributes.

www.ingramcontent.com/pod-product-compliance
Lightning Source LLC
LaVergne TN
LVHW091319080426
835510LV00007B/563